Discover Your Selling Advantage

FREE
Sales Personality Assessment

To obtain your FREE Sales Personality Assessment, log onto www.SellingforWomen.com and click on the **FREE Sales Personality Assessment button** on the homepage.

Use Reference # **Book ONE**

Or call 1-800-681-7808 Toll FREE for more details.

*This offer is open to all purchasers of *Lifestyle Selling for Women* by Pauline O'Malley and Brenda Page, CPC. The offer is limited to one Sales Personality Assessment per person and is subject to availability and/or changes to the offer. This is a limited time offer and the Assessment must be completed by the date shown on the electronic invitation. The value of the SellingforWomen. com Sales Personality Assessment is $175, as of September 2009. Corporate or organizational purchases may not use one book to invite more than two people. Participants in the Sales Personality Assessment are under no financial obligation whatsoever to Pauline O'Malley, Brenda Page, Lifestyle Selling for Women, SellingforWomen.com or TheRevenueBuilder®. Pauline O'Malley, Brenda Page, Lifestyle Selling for Women, SellingforWomen.com or TheRevenueBuilder® reserves the right to refuse admission to anyone it believes is outside the scope of this offer. For more information call 1-800-681-7808.

Lifestyle Selling
for Women

How to Sell More in
Less Time and Enjoy Life!

Pauline O'Malley and Brenda Page, CPC

Order this book online at www.trafford.com
or email orders@trafford.com

Most Trafford titles are also available at major online book retailers.

ILLUSTRATED BY
Mia Hansen

EDITED BY
Pauline Richards

COVER DESIGN/ARTWORK BY
Mia Hansen

Note for Librarians: A cataloguing record for this book is available from Library
and Archives Canada at www.collectionscanada.ca/amicus/index-e.html

Printed in Victoria, BC, Canada.

ISBN: 978-1-4251-4365-7 (soft)
ISBN: 978-1-4251-4366-4 (ebook)

*Our mission is to efficiently provide the world's finest, most comprehensive
book publishing service, enabling every author to experience success.
To find out how to publish your book, your way, and have it available
worldwide, visit us online at www.trafford.com*

Trafford rev. 9/21/2009

 www.trafford.com

North America & international
toll-free: 1 888 232 4444 (USA & Canada)
phone: 250 383 6864 ♦ fax: 812 355 4082

Praise for *Lifestyle Selling for Women*

"It's the clarity you bring that defines the difference."

~ **Norma Sebestyen, Merck**

"This system provided us a different discipline to approach clients and accept referrals. As a result, my assistant is no longer putting in the crazy hours he used to."

~ **Jane Russell, BA, CIM, FCSI, CFP, CSA, FMA,**
Investors Group Financial

"*Lifestyle Selling for Women* provides a logical progression to answer the question, *'What should I be doing now?'* The structure ties together prospecting, developing and closing in an intuitive way."

~ **Sandy Gerber & Karley Cunningham,**
3 Degrees West Communications

"Gives you a very practical model, and with the coaching sessions, it encourages you to actually practice and use what you learn."

~ **Kate Pelletier, British Columbia Institute of Technology**

"We had a really tough nut for a client, but after my sales representative followed the system, he won them over. Thank you for helping us grow our business!"

~ **Joyce Hayne, EMC Publications**

For our beautiful nieces,

Meara and Pearl

Contents

Note to Reader

When we identify gender differences in the book we will use generalizations. In other words, we refer to the majority in a group rather than every individual. An example is that women are shorter than men. We know this is not always the case, but generally it is.

We believe that women and men are more alike than they are different. For example, contrary to popular myth, women and men are equally good at navigating; they just take different paths to get to the same destination. Women tend to rely on landmarks, whereas men tend to use distance. One method is not necessarily better than the other; they are just different. Being different, depending on the situation you are in, can be an advantage, or a disadvantage.

Few books on selling incorporate the differences between the genders. We are not saying that one gender is better than the other. We are saying that generally there are some subtle and not so subtle differences between women and men that affect daily conversations and decision-making.

The truth is, each person is unique and should be treated as such.

Lifestyle Selling for Women is a Reality

For years, women have struggled with balancing work and life. Women are realizing that working hard will not take them to where they want to go. We are constantly looking for ways to streamline our efforts to find more time, and additional resources, to find that balance.

Lifestyle Selling for Women is more than a mindset, it is a reality. This proven step-by-step system is uniquely designed for women entrepreneurs and selling professionals. Based on the principles of TheRevenueBuilder® it breaks the entire sales process down into three simple steps.

By following these steps you will discover new ways to reach your desired goals, earn what you are truly worth and break through the barriers that may be hindering your success. You will experience not only sales results, but "lifestyle selling" results.

- You will naturally emit positive energy
- You will have more time for family and personal interests
- You will generate more income
- You will be proud of the money you make
- You will love what you do

Filled with facts, proven advice and links to website tools this guide will help you create that healthy balance.

 Download FREE tools at **www.SellingforWomen.com**

Call us Toll FREE at **1-800-681-7808**

Let's Start with the Facts

Since the Industrial Revolution, women's roles have been changing from working full-time in the home to working part-time or full-time in business and in the home. Sixty years ago, 29 percent of adult women worked outside the home. Today, 60 percent are in the workforce.[1]

Sales is one of the most rapidly expanding fields in the United States, with about 12 million people currently in sales positions. Ten to fifteen years ago few women were enrolled in sales courses. Today, women outnumber men in college sales courses.[2]

Women of all ages are increasingly turning to entrepreneurship. 70 percent of women in the United States are responsible for all private start ups[3] and more than 58 percent of corporate purchasing agents are women.[4]

In the United Kingdom, 70 percent of women started their business because they wanted more flexible working conditions. 75 percent said work-life balance is better when running your own business.[5]

In Canada, reports show that 60 percent of self-employed women are "Lifestylers," a term used to describe business owners who have chosen self-employment specifically to balance the demands of work and family.[6]

With such a significant increase in women entrepreneurs and sales professionals, it would follow that women have a significant impact on all purchasing decisions in both business and consumer markets.

Women Take Control

Over the past three years, 310 of every 100,000 immigrant women started a business, compared to 220 of every 100,000 of women born in the United States – a difference of 41 percent. Immigrant women are more likely to start their own business in order to have greater flexibility in raising their children and to avoid the barriers that exist in traditional employment.[7]

In the United States, nearly 10.4 million firms are owned by women.[8] Women in Canada make up the largest share of the self-employed workforce than any other country in the world.[9]

In the United States, between 1997 and 2006, the number of majority women-owned firms grew 42 percent, from 5.4 million to 7.7 million. When compared to all firms, which grew only 23 percent, predictions indicate that this trend shows no signs of slowing.[10]

Many women entrepreneurs are staying small because they want to. Of the companies exclusively women-owned, 81 percent are without employees.[11] The stress and demands of growing a small business into a giant one often conflicts with other priorities.

The same applies to women in employment. Often these women will pass up promotions or full-time employment to balance their work and personal lives.[12]

Where's the Balance

Another challenge women face in business involves their support system. Most businessmen are privileged enough to have a woman in their life who not only joins them in everyday fun and personal partnership, but also provides a great deal of support for their business. These women positively impact the success of these men.

Men traditionally have women in their lives to do the laundry, take care of the gardening, schedule doctor's appointments, pick up the dry cleaning, prepare meals, make sure the house is clean, take the primary role in caring for the children, throw parties to impress clients and sometimes assist in the business itself.

Seldom do you see husbands offering this kind of support for their working wives.[13] This is significant because 70 percent of Canadian female entrepreneurs are married and nearly one-third have children under the age of twelve.[14]

Being in business provides a unique means of control. It can shape the life of a person, both professionally and personally, in a very positive way. Women are increasingly taking advantage of the opportunity to be self-employed.

"Women want men, careers, money, children, friends, luxury,
comfort, independence, freedom, respect, love
and three-dollar panty hose that won't run."
~ Phyllis Diller, actress/comedian

Women in Sales

Many sales positions are similar to running a business. You can create your own schedule, enjoy flexible hours and avoid bumping into the glass ceiling of capped earnings. Women see sales as a tremendous opportunity because of these benefits and they are very good at it.

Women's natural style is not to push a sale, but rather to help individuals and companies solve their challenges and find appropriate solutions. Women typically don't want to impose or be aggressive in a sale; instead, women listen, ask questions, understand the client's challenges and offer solutions. The female approach focuses on the human connection involved in business and uses the initial meeting to understand a client's needs.

The key mandate of the female style is to build the relationship. Women take the time to tune into and hear the needs of their clients before preparing solutions. Women are also more prone to refer business elsewhere if their company cannot provide appropriate solutions, as business is truly about relationships.

"I think that women making no apology for being women is very refreshing."
~ Drew Barrymore, actress/producer

The Woman's Advantage

Many women are more right-brained than men[15], which means they tend to focus on relationship building and have strong listening skills, empathy and intuition. People who are relationship oriented and can empathize with others do well in sales.

The stereotypical male way of selling, with its focus on walking into a prospect's office knowing all the answers, can often block the goal that should be achieved - the sale. This method of selling is based on men's predominant use of left-brain, logical thinking.

Women, therefore, generally have a more natural ability in sales than men. Noticeably, in the last fifteen years, men in sales have begun to alter their sales style to one that is similar to that of women's styles.

"Our beliefs can move us forward in life
or they can hold us back."
~ Oprah Winfrey

Negotiating Your Worth

As women, we minimize what we're willing to ask for. This usually shows up when we're negotiating for money or perks. Fear or underestimating our worth can stop us from asking for more. We also tend to request only what we need, not what we want - unlike men, who tend to do the reverse.

When we don't approach negotiating from the same perspective as men, we inevitably lose out. For example, suppose that at the age of 22 an equally qualified man and woman receive job offers for $25,000 a year. The woman does not negotiate and accepts the job for $25,000. The man negotiates and gets his offer raised to $30,000.

Even if each of them receives identical 3 percent raises every year throughout their careers (which is unlikely), by the time they reach the age 60, the gap between their salaries will have widened to more than $15,000 a year, with the woman earning only $76,870 and the man earning $92,243.

While this may not seem like an enormous spread, remember that the man will have been making more all along, with extra earnings over the 38 years totaling $361,171. If the man had simply banked the difference every year in a savings account earning 3 percent interest, by the age of 60 he would have $568,834 more than the woman.

Your negotiation skills are required in any sales interaction, whether you are the seller or the one being sold to. The art of negotiation plays a role in your sales success.

The Function of Selling

The days of using the same sales speech for every client are over. Each client has their own set of challenges, just as women and men each have distinct communication and behavioral styles. The function of selling is to identify people's unique needs and help them achieve their desires.

You are "facilitating the buying process."

The word "facilitate" is derived from the French adjective *facile* which means "easy." It is important to make the buying experience as easy as possible.

Notice the word "buying." The context is in the client's, not yours. Your focus is 100 percent on the client, treating them as individuals, customizing your interaction with them, aware of their industry, their company challenges and perhaps, their personal issues. This attention will take your sales success up to the next level and decrease the time it normally takes to close a deal.

When you hear the word "process," you may think of systems, strategies or management. Selling is a step-by-step methodology, one that is clearly defined and easy to follow. The management of this process must incorporate benchmarks.

Three Simple Steps

The application of a proven system will make the buying experience easy and enjoyable.

Ensuring that it is simple will save precious time and increase revenues.

Let's break it down to three simple steps.

1. Define your Niche Market to determine who you want to do business with.

2. Identify your client's Level of Interest within 5 minutes of communicating with them.

3. Use the Nine Methods of Inspiration to encourage your clients to commit faster and more often.

The Three Steps to
LifestyleSelling

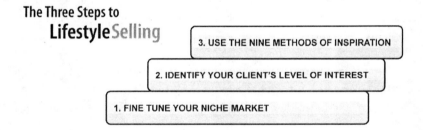

3. USE THE NINE METHODS OF INSPIRATION

2. IDENTIFY YOUR CLIENT'S LEVEL OF INTEREST

1. FINE TUNE YOUR NICHE MARKET

1. FINE TUNE YOUR NICHE MARKET

Define Your Niche Market

Your Niche Market is a group of future clients. These are the people who will most likely have a demand for your products and services. These are the people that you have identified to be the best fit for your solutions and your company.

Identifying who belongs in your Niche Market will save you tremendous time, energy and money.

Defining the parameters of your Niche Market will also help you find clients who are the best fit. Knowing what you want in a client will bring healthy, long-term relationships.

Determining who you do not want to do business with will result in a thriving business for many years to come. This is where many selling professionals and entrepreneurs make a mistake. They think their solution will suit everyone.

For example, extremely successful companies like *Estee Lauder* and *lululemon athletica* offer high quality products. These companies focus their attention on women who invest more on their personal image than most. They do not waste resources trying to attract a wider audience.

How to Identify Ideal Clients

You will have to ask yourself many questions along the path of lifestyle selling. The first question is: "Is this potential client in my Niche Market or not?"

The answer is either "yes" or "no."

The more you refine your Niche Market, the clearer your answer will be. It is important to define your Niche Market in a systematic manner so that you include people and companies with whom it is worthwhile to do business and exclude those who are not.

Follow these four steps to identify your ideal clients:

1. Explore challenges clients face.
2. Define your company's solutions.
3. Match clients' challenges with your company's solutions.
4. Focus your specialty.

Identify Ideal Clients

STEP 4: Focus on Your Specialty

STEP 3: Match Clients' Challenges with Your Company's Solutions

STEP 2: Define Your Company's Solutions

STEP 1: Explore Challenges Clients Face

STEP 1: Explore Challenges Clients Face

People buy to solve a problem or fill a need. Focusing on a client's problem is the best place to start when identifying who your ideal clients are.

Challenges that relate to consumers could include "high gas prices," "losing weight" or "the downturn in the economy."

Challenges that relate to companies could include "remaining competitive," "a tight hiring market," "fluctuating currencies" or "fast turnaround."

Make a list of all the challenges that your clients are experiencing right now. Don't think about what your business has to offer. Open your mind to their world and their needs.

   www.SellingforWomen.com

Challenges Clients Face
□
□
□
□
□
□
□
□
□

STEP 2: Define Your Company's Solutions

Now, clear your head of your clients' challenges and focus on your company's solutions. These are made up of products and services. A product is a tangible solution, like "photocopiers." Your services are intangibles such as "24-hour delivery" or a "60 minute facial."

Make a list of all your current products and services, every single one of them.

  www.SellingforWomen.com

Your Company's Solutions
□
□
□
□
□
□
□
□
□
□
□

STEP 3: Match Clients' Challenges with Your Company's Solutions

Match each challenge from your list in Step 1 with your products and services listed in Step 2.

For example, if the challenge is "fast turnaround" the solution could be "24-hour delivery."

Another example of a challenge could be "tired-looking skin." The solution could be "a 60-minute facial."

Do not try to force a match with all of your clients' challenges with solutions. Remain objective. You may be surprised by the results.

 www.SellingforWomen.com

Challenges Clients Face	Your Company's Solutions

What Did You Discover?

Some of your solutions may not be assigned to any of your clients' challenges? Perhaps these solutions are not essential any longer. They may be out of date. If so, think about discontinuing them.

Some of your clients' challenges may not be matched with a solution. Or they may be matched with a feeble solution that will not completely resolve their problem. You may have to rethink how you meet your clients' needs. Consider rolling out a new product or service, or bundle your existing solutions to create a new one.

When your company's solution solves a client's problem, you both win.

*"Only through trial and suffering
is the soul strengthened."*

~ Helen Keller, author

STEP 4: Focus On Your Specialty

A specialist can be defined as someone who has an in-depth understanding of their client base within specific industries. For example, someone with an education in finance may focus exclusively on the financial services sector and target banks and credit unions as their potential clients. A former dental assistant may do well in the pharmaceutical industry.

Focusing on your specialty is the ideal scenario, but this is not always possible. You may have years of sales experience, but perhaps not in the industry you now represent. You may be relatively new to the employment world. If you do not have a specialty in any particular industry, focus on the top industry sectors with which you are familiar.

Here are some examples of general industry sectors.

General Industry Sectors	
Accounting	Government
Architecture	Healthcare
Auto	Hospitality
Construction	Manufacturing
Distribution	Real Estate
Education	Retail
Financial	Technology
Food	Warehouse

Having trouble identifying your specialty? Think about one of your hobbies or interests to get you started. For instance, a passion for home decorating may lead to a specialty in home improvement contracting or real estate. Still stuck? What activities have you enjoyed in the past? These are the industry sectors where you can be perceived as a specialist.

Choose at least two industry sectors where you think you may have some expertise, or at least some general knowledge.

Selling is more enjoyable when you match your education, expertise and vocabulary with an industry sector where there is a good fit.

Now that you have identified the challenges that your clients face and the solutions that you offer that may be a good fit, let's take it a step further.

> *"Everyone has a talent, what is rare is the courage to follow*
> *the talent to the dark place where it leads."*
> *~ Erica Jong, novelist/poet*

Fine Tune Your Niche Market

Let's suppose you've just attended a networking function and have collected a stack of business cards. You may think that they are all your potential clients.

Use the following five steps to determine whether or not clients belong in your Niche Market:

1. Understand your existing clients.

2. Define your General Niche Market parameters.

3. Narrow the parameters even more.

4. Ensure success with the best.

5. Source high quality clients.

Fine Tuning Your Niche Market

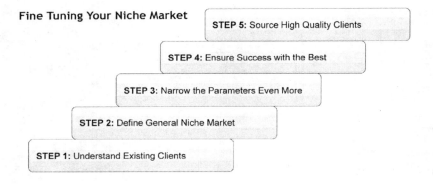

STEP 5: Source High Quality Clients

STEP 4: Ensure Success with the Best

STEP 3: Narrow the Parameters Even More

STEP 2: Define General Niche Market

STEP 1: Understand Existing Clients

STEP 1: Understand Existing Clients

The better you know your clients, the better equipped you will be to anticipate their needs and provide them with solutions.

Conduct research, prior to talking to your clients directly, to find out what has changed recently in their lives.

Here are some points to consider.

  www.SellingforWomen.com

Research Check List
1. What is the client's website address?
2. What are the client's specific products and services?
3. What do the online newswire and financial credit services say?
4. What are the client's key markets?
5. Who are the client's key competitors?
6. What are the client's revenue and profit trends?
7. If it is a public traded company, how do the client's financials compare with those of similar companies?
8. What are the client's industry challenges?
9. Is their market growing or shrinking?
10. What's changing?

You don't have to answer all of these questions but the more you know the better prepared you'll be when introducing yourself to a client. Searching the Internet, or visiting your Chamber of Commerce or your local library will provide you with good insight into your client's world.

After you have obtained some general information about your client and their industry, conducting market research surveys will help to understand your client's specific buying behaviors.

Before asking your client directly, try to answer each of the following questions to determine how well you know them. If you can't answer a question completely, don't guess or assume the answer.

Instead, be aware that research is required.

www.SellingforWomen.com

Questions to Ask Yourself

1. Where are your clients located? Where are their head offices? Where are the Decision Makers located? (Locally, nationally, overseas?)

2. Where do your clients shop? (Locally, overseas, the Internet?)

3. How do your clients buy? (Telephone, the Internet, in person?)

4. What do your clients buy? What are considered commodity items? What are the specialty items?

5. What do your clients need? What are the essential ingredients that keep their businesses thriving? What can they not live without?

6. What challenges do your clients face?

7. What are your clients' goals? What do they have planned for the future?

8. What funding range or spending limit do your clients have?

9. When do your clients expect delivery? (Same day, next day, seven days?) When is their busy season? Their slow season?

10. What is changing in your client's life? Do you know?

11. What would consistently make your clients feel special? (Answer this question only if you have talked about it with them.)

Do You Really Understand Your Clients?

Did you discover that you don't know as much about your clients as you thought?

When you visit your clients, do you take the time to get to know them? Do you give the same presentation to every potential client, or do you customize presentations according to their individual challenges and goals?

If you don't really know your clients on an in-depth business level, you may miss an opportunity to offer them solutions that fit, which could cost you the sale.

"Women tend to be more goal-oriented than men. Women have a much larger set of aims and many of those goals are not necessarily congruent or even complementary to building a business. For example, women have much more empathy for the needs of others than do men and they allocate more time, emotion and economic resources to noble pursuits."
~ Millionaire Women Next Door,
Thomas J. Stanley, Ph.D

STEP 2: Define General Niche Market

To define your Niche Market in general terms, location is a good place to start. For example, if you are based in Chicago selling financial planning services that require at least two face-to-face meetings with clients every year, one of your Niche Market parameters would be "the City of Chicago" and maybe its nearby suburbs. Depending on how your clients buy, the parameter might be different. For instance, your geographic parameter may be "the world" if their needs can be met via the Internet.

> **Hint:**   *Ask yourself how your clients prefer to buy. Over the phone, via the Internet, face-to-face or a combination? Are they comfortable not seeing any one at all? Once a year? Twice maybe? Is there enough profit built into your solution to travel if you have to? Knowing how your clients prefer to buy will help you decide what delivery mechanism best serves them, which will help you determine where you need to focus.*

It's best to start with a Niche Market that has narrow parameters and then expand them as you grow. Ask yourself, "How can I narrow the features of my Niche Market to enable me to concentrate on clients who are the best match?" Time equals money, so spend it with people that meet your criteria to obtain the highest return on your investment of time and money.

General Niche Market Features

The following points will help you narrow and define your Niche Market. Some may not apply to your business, but they are all important to consider. Note: In a few years your Niche Market may change.

www.SellingforWomen.com

General Niche Market Features
1. Geographic territory: Countries are large. Consider specific states, provinces and cities.
2. Size of company: By number of employees and by revenue. We recommend that you use both.
3. Ownership/corporate status: Small office/home office, public, private, non-profit or government.
4. Location of headquarters: Very important if your solution requires the ultimate authority of the CEO or President.
5. Years in business: You may wish to deal only with companies that have been in business for many years unless they are heavily financed.
6. Age groups: Generally applies to the consumer market.
7. Gender: Generally applies to the consumer market.
8. Specialty industries: Industries where you have a deeper understanding.
9. Fast-growing industries: For example, telecommunication, biotech, health and film.
10. Title/position of individuals: Always start at the top. CEOs and Presidents decide who their long-term partners will be.
11. Stage of company: Start-up, capital acquisition, mature.
12. Credit rating: On-line reports and other qualified assurances of liquidity.

STEP 3: Narrow the Parameters Even More

Many major corporations have large marketing and sales departments. The function of these departments include advertising, communications, proposal writing, prospecting, cold calling, reviewing requests for proposals, conducting Needs Assessments and closing the deal. They have the resources to handle many clients at once.

However, of the 5.4 million firms in the United States, 75 percent do not have employees. Of the firms within this total that are exclusively women-owned, 81 percent are without employees.[16]

When you're an independent businesswoman who is 100 percent responsible for revenue building it may be unreasonable for you to market to hundreds of thousands of potential clients. You must have adequate resources to tend to the needs of your clients so they will not become dissatisfied and do business elsewhere.

You can start with as many as 500 potential clients in your Niche Market or as few as 100. For example, one of our clients is a new technology solutions provider with four partners and no employees. One of the partners is responsible for sales. Because the company is small it only needs to close one deal a month, but they have to be substantial in size. Therefore, she has decided to market exclusively to the largest 100 companies with head offices located in her city. To narrow the market parameters even more, she concentrates only on the company's most senior Decision Makers. *That's* target marketing!

STEP 4: Ensure Success with the Best

It is important to keep narrowing the parameters of your Niche Market to prevent becoming overwhelmed. Is there anything else that will narrow the features of your Niche Market?

Whether you start with 100 or 100,000 potential clients in your Niche Market, they have to perfectly match your company's solutions and resources. These are the potential buyers who will eventually say "yes."

Be clear about what you *don't* want. Write down the qualities you do not want to attract; for example, "overly demanding," "extremely negative" and "insufficient income to pay promptly."

Sadly, we may forget to avoid these negative qualities and pay for it later. Difficult clients consume our time and resources and bring stress and negative energy to our work environment.

"I'm not a sponge exactly, but I find that
something new I look at is a great opportunity for ideas."
~ Martha Stewart

STEP 5: Source High Quality Clients

Now that you know what you're looking for, where do you find these high quality clients? Consider the following resources.

List Acquisitions

We are fans of list acquisition - but proceed with caution. A list acquisition company requires months to acquire, publish, sell and distribute data. Therefore, some lists are 12 to 18 months old.

To accelerate your revenue building activities, get the names, titles, direct telephone numbers and email addresses of the most current Decision Makers.

Make sure the list acquisition service you use is reputable and guarantees the quality of the data. They should be consulting with you to help you find your ideal clients.

Hint: *Aim high! There is nothing more powerful than having the top Decision Maker refer you to the person who is in charge of the acquisition of your solutions. CEOs, Presidents and VPs may be the only contacts you wish to speak with initially. If, for instance, you are a Consultant, Managers within that company may view you as their competition. However, their bosses see you as an impartial outsider.*

Newspapers

Newspapers, either online or paper, are a great place to find high quality clients for little or no cost. Look in the classified section since companies that are hiring are often growing. Read the business section to find companies that are making changes; change is opportunity. Articles can also reveal who the most recent Decision Makers are.

Local newspapers are a fabulous resource for up-to-date information on the movers and shakers within a business community. Consider subscribing to online versions of periodicals in your targeted markets.

The Internet

Check your preferred local, national and international news services online at least once a week to see where opportunities may be.

When researching your Niche Market clients on the Internet, read the press releases on their website first to find out what is happening, or is projected to happen. Here you will see who the Decision Makers are. The Contact Us page will sometimes help to uncover additional Decision Makers and personnel who influence the company's strategies.

Magazines

Think about joining associations that your clients belong to. Many have their own magazine publications that highlight the prominent leaders in their industries.

Subscribe to industry-specific magazines that your clients read, or check if your local library subscribes to these publications. Scan the "who's who" pages and look for advertisers who may wish to buy from you.

Networking Groups

Almost 40 per cent of women sole proprietors in Canada are members of a trade association. This is at twice the rate of men.[17]

Women join networking groups and associations 50 percent more than men do.[18]

Attending networking meetings and using the membership lists of these associations are great ways to find clients. Look for networking groups that fit your industry. Keep your business cards handy because you never know where you will meet a new client. Share your Niche Market parameters with others so they will refer specific clients to you. Women generally feel an allegiance to fellow women and often provide referrals.

Conferences and Trade Fairs

Ninety-four percent of corporations send representatives to women's business conferences and trade fairs.[19] Use these events to find high quality clients.

Referrals

Where is the best place to find high quality clients? Your current clients.

Satisfied clients should refer business to you on an ongoing basis. Don't be afraid to ask for referrals from clients who are not currently giving them to you.

When your clients understand the parameters of your Niche Market, they are more likely to introduce you to friends and colleagues who can become your high quality clients as well.

Now that you have defined your Niche Market, it's time to identify your client's Level of Interest.

2. IDENTIFY YOUR CLIENT'S LEVEL OF INTEREST

The Six Levels of Interest

Psychologists agree that all human beings go through stages before they become advocates of a new idea or concept.[20] After years of development and testing, we discovered that clients go through Six Levels of Interest before they become an advocate of a particular product or service.

Each Level of Interest identifies how accepting a person is to doing business with you.

 www.SellingforWomen.com

Level	Definition
Level I Exist	These clients have no intention of trying something new.
Level 2 Think	These clients are considering a change.
Level 3 Plan	These clients now intend to take action.
Level 4 Do	These clients are actively engaged in resolving their challenge or fulfilling a need.
Level 5 Buy	These clients need their buying decision validated.
Level 6 Believe	These clients are advocates.

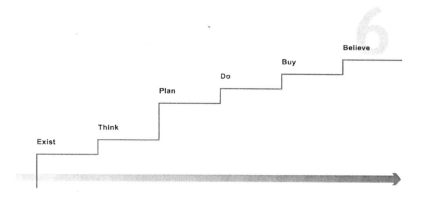

The Buying Process

People buy because they have a problem to resolve or a need to fulfill. Therefore, all people go through a clearly defined process to alleviate their challenge or fulfill their desire.

To better understand the buying process, let's examine the public acceptance of the automated teller machine. The first cash dispensing machine was developed in 1939 in New York City by the Citibank of New York. It was removed after six months due to lack of client acceptance.

When they were redesigned and reinstalled in the early 1990's, most people did not use ATMs. Today, this is no longer the case. People who now use the machine are in Level 5 Buy. People who use ATMs exclusively and never set foot in a bank are in Level 6 Believe. They changed their behavior enough to become advocates of the technology.

Some people still prefer to wait in line until a bank teller can serve them. They don't believe they need to deal with ATMs. They simply don't want to change. These folks are in Level 1 Exist.

Can you convert someone in Level 1 Exist to move up to Level 6 Believe in one interaction? No. It takes many impressions to inspire prospects to become clients. Reducing the number of these interactions accelerates the selling process. Assessing your client's exact Level of Interest will cut down the number of interactions and inspire your client to commit faster.

You want all of your clients to become Level 6 "Believers" so that they will tell potential clients about their positive experiences with you.

Ensure that your clients are aware of your solutions throughout your entire relationship with them.

> *"When the right things are done,*
> *the right things will come."*
> *~ Kari Yuers, CEO*
> *The Kryton Group of Companies*

Level 1 Exist

Clients who have no intention of trying something new.

These clients are:

- Unaware that there might be a problem
- Uninformed about the long-term consequences of their behavior
- Not interested in thinking about the problem
- Often defensive in response to a new idea
- Often demoralized about their inability to change

Clients in Level 1 Exist are probably not interested in speaking with you. They might have just bought from someone else. They might be happy with their current vendor or they may not be aware that a challenge exists. However, they are potential clients that you have chosen to be in your Niche Market.

Counting on the premise that change is constant, if these clients don't have a problem now, they eventually will.

"While women control slightly more than half the wealth now, it will be a tsunami over the next 15 to 20 years."
~ Martha Barletta, Founder, TrendSight

Level 2 Think

Clients who are aware that a problem may exist and are considering a change.

These clients are:

- Actively seeking information
- Beginning to consider doing things differently
- Talking and listening
- Assessing the pros and cons of change

Responses from Level 2 Think clients include, "Really? What else does your product do?" Or, "How would you see that working for us?" Buyers in Level 2 Think are checking your website and those of your competitors, gathering brochures and collecting data. They are beginning to form an intent to act.

Warning!   *Clients in Level 2 Think can remain here indefinitely. They will collect information for months, sometimes years. They never seem to be able to make a commitment. However, with the right tools, they can be inspired to move forward.*

Level 3 Plan

Clients who intend to take action on a predetermined date.

These clients have:

- Developed a plan of action
- Set goals
- Gathered definitive information
- Established a timeline and are facing a critical deadline

To determine the difference between clients in Level 2 Think and Level 3 Plan, ask yourself, "Have I found out what their deadline is?" "Does the acquisition of a new solution depend upon meeting a certain deadline?" "Can we resolve their challenge in time?" If the answer to any of these questions is "no," they are not in Level 3 Plan.

Heads up!   *Clients in Level 3 Plan are in a transitional stage. They want to change quickly, so stay in touch.*

Level 4 Do

Clients who are actively engaged in resolving the challenge or fulfilling the need.

These clients have:

- Accepted the change process
- Appointed resources to specific tasks
- Allocated the funds
- A critical deadline to meet

Warning!   *Of all the Levels of Interest, clients in Level 4 Do are the most susceptible to slipping back.*

Picture this scenario. You have just made the deal of the century. You rush back to the office, completely elated. You tell everyone, "I got the deal!" Then someone asks, "Yeah, but did you get the check?" You respond, "No, but I'll get it." Weeks go by and your calls and emails go unanswered and you still don't have the check.

What happened?

The client has either chosen not to buy or has purchased from the competition.

The process of change is dynamic. Clients move up and down the Six Levels of Interest throughout the entire buying process. This is why it's important to accurately determine your client's Level of Interest - *every time* you interact with them.

Level 5 Buy

Clients who need their buying decision validated.

You have made the sale when you have:

- A signed contract

- An outline of specific expectations

- 100 percent of the payment

Clients in Level 5 Buy are not necessarily 100 percent committed. They may be experiencing regret about their decision. Others around them may be questioning their thought processes. Either way, beware of buyer's remorse.

Clients in Level 5 Buy need to have their buying decision validated until the symptoms of buyer's remorse pass. They are relying on you to remind them why they invested in the first place. It's imperative to reassure your client that their decision was a wise one.

Hint: *To save time and streamline the decision-making process, ensure that your final proposal also serves as your contractual agreement. The final proposal should ideally outline exactly what the client's expectations are to fulfill the contract. It should also stipulate what you require from the client to guarantee successful delivery of your solution.*

Level 6 Believe

Clients who are advocates.

These clients:

- Continue to purchase from you
- Refer business to you on a regular basis
- Have regular contact with you
- Have developed a relationship with you
- Are 100 percent loyal

This is the Level that you want all of your clients to be – sooner rather than later.

"To keep the lamp burning you have to
keep putting oil in it."
~ Mother Theresa

Assess Your Client's Level of Interest

A potential client who has never heard of you before is in Level 1 Exist. A client in Level 4 Do wants to resolve their issue quickly. They both require different solutions, dialogue and tools to inspire them to commit to the next level.

The question is how do you determine the difference between a client in Level 1 and a client in Level 4 so that you know how to treat them?

You just need two tools:

1.   The Interaction Questionnaire.
2.   The Interaction Scorecard.

It is important to assign your clients a Level of Interest each and every time you interact with them.

Your client's Level of Interest will change right before your eyes. In one conversation you may find out that they think you are the greatest solution provider in the world. In the next, they stop providing you with business.

Your Interaction Questionnaire will help you uncover which Level of Interest they are currently in and why the change occurred.

The Interaction Scorecard will provide you with an objective overview of the opportunity in that moment of time.

The Interaction Questionnaire

Use the following five steps to build your own Interaction Questionnaire:

1. Prepare.

2. Develop Perceived Fit questions.

3. Develop questions to discover Decision Makers and Influencers.

4. Develop Critical Deadline questions.

5. Develop Allocation of Funds questions.

Build Your Interaction Questionnaire

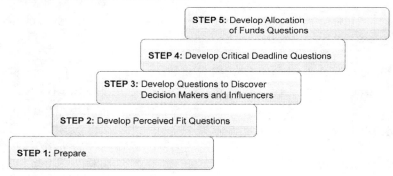

Interaction Questionnaire Example

www.SellingforWomen.com

The Four Keys	Questions
Perceived Fit Does the client perceive a fit with us?	What do you wish to accomplish? What are your challenges? What are the most important solutions that you require? What key qualities are most important to you? How have you accomplished this task in the past?
Decision Maker Who are the Decision Makers and Influencers and what is their decision-making process?	What is your role in this project? What is your decision-making process? Who else is involved in the decision-making process? Who else is involved in the implementation of the solution? Which outside consultants do you plan to have working on this project with you? Which department is driving this project? Who is ultimately responsible?

www.SellingforWomen.com

The Four Keys	Questions
Critical Deadline Is there a critical deadline and can we meet it?	How long have you been looking for a solution? When do you need to make this decision? When would you like everything completed? What is your schedule for implementation? What is driving the dates? What outside influences could affect the schedule? What will happen if you don't make this decision?
Funds Allocated Are funds currently allocated?	When is your fiscal year-end? How much do you typically like to invest? What funds are currently allocated to this project? What is your fund allocation process? Our solutions range anywhere from $_____ to $_____. How does this fit with your requirements?

STEP 1: Prepare

A carefully crafted Interaction Questionnaire will enable you to quickly obtain information to determine your client's Level of Interest.

Most clients are impressed when your questions uncover facts about them and their business creating an "Ah Ha" moment. The quality of your questions will demonstrate to your client that you are listening intently, that you are a qualified specialist and that you truly want to solve their problems.

How you craft your questions will determine your success.

Open-Ended versus Closed-Ended Questions

Closed-ended questions leave you with "yes" or "no" answers. Often they do not provide the most accurate information from your client.

Open-ended questions, on the other hand, help to uncover the truth by opening-up the conversation. To do so, begin questions with:

- How
- What
- Where
- Who
- When

Notice the absence of "Why?"

"Why?" can invite defensiveness or insecurity. When emotions kick in, answers may not be reliable. When you are stuck in an

Interview or wish to press a point, ask "How come?" You may be surprised by the positive results.

Open the Conversation Even More

Begin your questions with:

- Help me understand . . .
- Out of curiosity . . .
- Tell me more about . . .
- Could you elaborate . . .

Don't let your clients talk too long or get off track. If this happens, say something like:

- Speaking of _____ , tell me more about . . .
- Back to _____ , could you elaborate on . . .

It's Not What You Say, It's How You Say It!

It's worthwhile to mention that as soon as your tone carries any level of judgment, anger, resentment or attack, listeners will become defensive, no matter what words you use. This defensiveness on behalf of your client may not be conscious, but it will have an impact on your success.

Preparing your questions is important, but if you deliver them in a brash manner, you may hit a wall. You may think you're being professional, but you could come across as "cold" and "hard."

In some industries being blunt does not necessarily mean being brusque. It may mean that you like to get to the point.

It is important to match your interview style with your Niche Market to ensure further success.

On the other hand, when your tone is sincere, curious and understanding, listeners will engage with you. When people perceive you as sincere and you demonstrate that you care, you will establish a positive rapport quickly with them.

STEP 2: Develop Perceived Fit Questions

Does the client perceive a fit with us?

Ask a few carefully crafted questions to explore the client's challenges, wants, needs and desires. For example, when conducting a meeting with a client, you may ask:

- What do you wish to accomplish?
- What are your challenges?
- What are the most important solutions that you require?
- What key qualities are most important to you?
- How have you accomplished this task in the past?

STEP 3: Develop Questions to Discover Decision Makers and Influencers

Who are the Decision Makers and Influencers and what is their decision-making process?

Decision Makers are those who ultimately have the power to spend the money. Influencers are those who affect the outcome. Some decisions require more than one Decision Maker.

It is important to find out who you are dealing with: A Decision-Maker or an Influencer. In many companies, decisions are made by consensus. CEOs and Presidents rely on informed decisions made by the people around them.

The best way to reveal the Decision Makers and Influencers is to ask, "What is your decision-making process?" This will help you uncover who will influence and ultimately who will make the decision to buy.

The list of Decision Makers and Influencers may become larger or smaller over time. Track the titles and responsibilities of all Decision Makers and Influencers who could be involved during the buying process.

Hint: *The hierarchy of decision-making can also be influenced by the gender in charge. The male style of management - called command and control - involves top-down decision-making. The people at the top know best and tell everyone else what to do. Women, on the other hand, tend to be interactive leaders, basing decisions on who has the most information and sharing power.*[21]

Here are some questions that you can ask to uncover your client's decision-making process and reveal who the Decision Makers and Influencers could be:

What is your role in this project?

- What is your decision-making process?
- Who else is involved in the decision-making process?
- Who else is involved in the implementation of the solution?
- Which outside consultants do you plan to have working on this project with you?
- Which department is driving this project?
- Who is ultimately responsible?

Hint: *To demonstrate to your client that your relationship is based on mutual collaboration, state "As your partner on this project, it is really important that we are involved with all of the Decision Makers."*

STEP 4: Develop Critical Deadline Questions

Is there a critical deadline and can we meet it?

Determining your client's timeline requires discovering the milestones along their road when making a purchase. For instance, your client may require training after the contract is signed. The training could take up to five weeks. The milestone would be the completion of the training.

Milestones on the Road

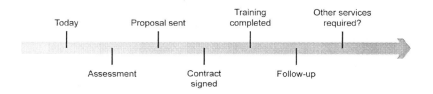

From the time you first meet with your client, to the time they sign the contract, how long does it take to close a deal? Three weeks? Six months?

Does this period of time match the date the client requires delivery of the solution? Do you have enough time to deliver the best solution? Determining these details early in the client relationship is critical to your success.

List all the tasks required to close a significant deal.

Then list the time range required to complete each task. At the bottom of your list, add-up the time it will take to close a sale. These are the Milestones along the Road that will help to uncover your client's critical deadline.

  www.SellingforWomen.com

Milestones Along the Road	Time Range for Each Task
	Total Time:

The following are examples of questions to help you uncover the critical deadline:

- How long have you have been looking for a solution?
- When do you need to make this decision?
- When would you like everything completed?
- What is your schedule for implementation?
- What is driving the dates?
- What outside influences could affect the schedule?
- What will happen if you don't make this decision?

Hint: *"When is your fiscal year end?" serves as a bridge between Critical Deadline questions and Funds Allocated questions.*

STEP 5: Develop Allocation of Funds Questions

Are funds currently allocated?

Talking about money in the first conversation with your client can be difficult. In some social circles, it is considered impolite. In business, however, talking about money is essential.

You must determine if money has been set aside for the investment today.

The following are Allocation of Funds questions to consider:

- When is your fiscal year-end?
- How much do you typically like to invest?
- What funds are currently allocated to this project?
- What is your fund allocation process?
- Our solutions range anywhere from $_____ to $ _____. How does this fit your requirements?

Avoid the word "budget" when crafting questions about the allocation of funds. The word budget may instill defensiveness in your client's mind. Instead, open up the dialogue to uncover possibilities of where your client might get the funding with words like "investment," "financing" and "resources."

Hint: *Money can always be found when value is perceived. You need to know if the funds are available now and how long they will be available in order to put a definitive "yes" or "no" on your Interaction Scorecard.*

The Interaction Scorecard

The Interaction Scorecard is a snapshot of your client's interpretation of their business in that particular moment of time. The accuracy of your Interaction Scorecard depends on three factors

1. The clarity of your questions

2. Your understanding of your client's situation

3. A crystal clear "yes" or "no" answer to the questions in the Four Keys of your Interaction Scorecard

 www.SellingforWomen.com

The Four Keys	Questions to Ask Yourself
Perceived Fit	Does the client perceive a fit with us?
Decision Maker	Who are the Decision Makers and Influencers and what is their decision-making process?
Critical Deadline	Is there a critical deadline and can we meet it?
Funds Allocated	Are funds currently allocated?

Interaction Scorecard Example

The following is an example of a completed Interaction Scorecard.

Date: June 30, 2009

Company: ACME COMPANY

Opportunity: Plastics Project

Potential Revenue: $150,000   **Fiscal Year-End:** Sept 30

The Four Keys	President	VP	CEO
Perceived Fit	Y	Y	Y
Decision Maker	Y	Y	Y
Critical Deadline	N	Y	Y
Funds Allocated	N	N	Y
LEVEL OF INTEREST	2	3	4
LEVEL OF OPPORTUNITY	2		

Heads Up: *Never assume that the person who signs the check is the only Decision Maker. Decision Makers rely on each other to come to an agreement about who will solve their problem.*

Assign the Level of Interest

In the Interaction Scorecard example, there are three people involved in the sale, all of which are Decision Makers. Their individual Level of Interest is determined by the "yes" or "no" answer in each of the Four Keys.

In the example below, the President has a "yes" beside Perceived Fit and a "yes" beside Decision Maker, but a "no" beside Critical Deadline and a "no" beside Funds Allocated. Therefore, she is in Level 2 Think.

Interaction Scorecard™

The Four Keys	Yes	No
Perceived Fit	✓	
Decision Maker	✓	
Critical Deadline		✗
Funds Allocated		✗

In the example below, the VP has a "yes" beside Perceived Fit, Decision Maker and Critical Deadline and a "no" beside Funds Allocated. She is in Level 3 Plan.

Interaction Scorecard™

The Four Keys	Yes	No
Perceived Fit	✓	
Decision Maker	✓	
Critical Deadline	✓	
Funds Allocated		✗

In the example below, the CEO perceives a fit, has a critical deadline and has allocated the funds to take action. She is in Level 4 Do.

Interaction Scorecard™

The Four Keys	Yes	No
Perceived Fit	✓	
Decision Maker	✓	
Critical Deadline	✓	
Funds Allocated	✓	

The Level of the Opportunity

Referring to only the Decision Makers, use the mathematical principle called "the lowest common denominator" to calculate the overall Level of Interest for the opportunity. Disregard the Influencers. Influencers don't have the authority to spend the money, so they are not calculated into the Level of Interest for the Opportunity.

In our Acme Company example, the Level of Interest for the plastics project Opportunity is Level 2 Think.

LEVEL OF OPPORTUNITY	2

Hint: *Influencers are placed on the Interaction Scorecard because they affect the decision-making process and they can be promoted up to Decision Maker any time.*

Predicting the Future

Forecasting future sales enables you to prioritize your time, anticipate cash flow requirements and hit your financial targets or maybe even surpass them. Each Level of Opportunity has a probability of closing.

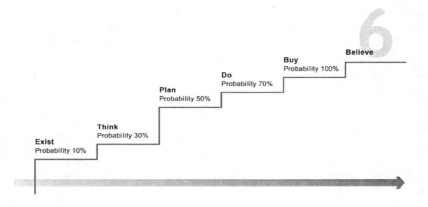

As shown in the diagram, Opportunities assessed at Level 1 Exist have a 10 percent probability of closing. Opportunities in Level 2 Think have a 30 percent chance of closing. Opportunities in Level 3 Plan are predicted to close 50 percent of the time and Opportunities that are assessed at Level 4 Do have a 70 percent chance of turning into a deal.

In the Acme Company example, the Opportunity for the plastics project sale is Level 2 Think, which has a 30 percent chance to close. The projected revenue for the sale is $150,000. Therefore, $45,000 is forecasted as potential revenue.

Prioritize

Review the matrix below. Opportunities assessed at Level 4 Do should receive first priority. We suggest that you then work on Level 3 Plan Opportunities followed by Level 2 Think. Don't ignore Opportunities in Level 1 Exist. They are important for future revenues.

PRIORITY	1	2	3	4
Perceived Fit	Y	Y	Y	Y
Decision Maker	Y	Y	Y	Y
Critical Deadline	Y	Y	N	N
Funds Allocated	Y	N	Y	N
LEVEL OF OPPORTUNITY	4	3	2	2

Focus on the Tools

Now that you have the tools to accurately determine the Level of Interest of each and every client, let's explore the Nine Methods of Inspiration that will encourage your clients to buy from you again and again.

"Those who are blessed with the most talent don't necessarily outperform everyone else. It's the people with follow-through who excel."
~ Mary Kay Ash, Mary Kay Cosmetics

3. USE THE NINE METHODS OF INSPIRATION

The Nine Methods of Inspiration

The Nine Methods of Inspiration are:

1.   Social

2.   Data

3.   Vision

4.   Emotion

5.   Commitment

6.   Replacement

7.   Environment

8.   Reward

9.   Help

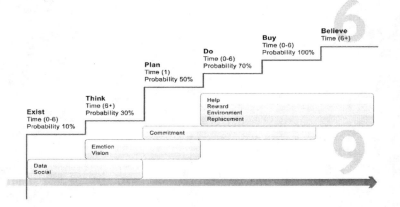

The Nine Methods of Inspiration

The Nine Methods of Inspiration support the entire revenue building process: marketing, selling and customer service.

Each Method will evoke the completion of a task. For instance, your client will open an envelope, make a phone call, fill out a form or sign a contract. The completion of these tasks will encourage your clients to move up the Six Levels of Interest.

Your role is to inspire positive and lasting change, but only when the change fulfills the desires and needs of your clients. Your objective is to affect people's behavior, knowledge and core beliefs with the Nine Methods of Inspiration.

Positive change occurs when The Nine Methods of Inspiration are translated into tools. These tools will inspire your clients to complete an activity.

This behavior will help your clients move up the Level of Interest in the buying process.

"Everyone needs to be valued.
Everyone has the potential to give something back."
~ Diana Princess of Wales

Tools That Inspire

Tools That Inspire

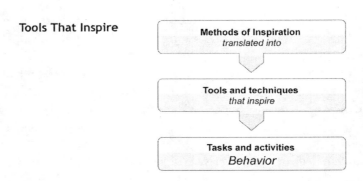

Heads up!   Each Method of Inspiration is effective only in certain Levels of Interest. Don't use all nine in each level. Use the Method that is appropriate for each Level of Interest in the order that they are presented.

The following pages define each of The Nine Methods. Below each definition are examples of tools that relate to the method.

1. Social

Legislative or cultural laws that affect behaviour.

The Social Method of Inspiration is effective in moving clients in Level 1 Exist to Level 2 Think.

Legislative Laws

Laws affect client's behavior. Anyone who owns a car must purchase a minimum amount of liability insurance dictated by a governing body. The minute we buy a car, we are obligated to speak to an insurance agent.

Industry Standards

Bylaws, codes and restrictions influence how business is done. When you buy a lamp in the United States it is UL or CA approved in accordance with the *Consumer Protection Act*. In Canada, it must be either CUL or CSA registered. Either way, the store that purchased the lamp to sell to you is restricted by these standards. What standards must your clients adhere to when making purchase decisions?

Third-Party Test Results

Test results from well-known and reputable sources are difficult to dispute. Examples include engineering specifications and market research studies.

Loss Leaders

Loss leaders are goods and services sold either at a loss or slightly above margin to encourage us to do business with a particular establishment.

Referrals

A referral can influence a client's buying behavior, particularly if it is from a friend or a colleague in the same industry.

The Woman's Advantage

When buying cars, most people underestimate the buying power of women. Women influence 95 percent of all auto purchases. Women purchase 65 percent of all new cars and 53 percent of all used cars.[22] Therefore, when purchasing vehicle insurance women are more often affected by legislative law than men. What's interesting to note is that 39 percent of women would rather deal with female sales professionals. Only 10 percent of men actually prefer dealing with a man.[23]

"My ambition is to be happy."
~ Penelope Cruz, actress

2. Data

Information that increases awareness.

The following examples illustrate how the Data Method of Inspiration helps to move clients in Level 1 Exist to Level 2 Think.

Advertising

You see an ad in the paper for a furniture sale at a store you've never heard of. The exact dining room table you've been looking for is on sale. The ad provides the store's address, a map and a telephone number. You may be inspired to visit the showroom.

Brochures

A carefully crafted brochure or one-page information sheet may not make the phone ring, but it will provide potential buyers with memory cues. It can also inspire them to write down the information for future use.

Mailing Lists

Ask your clients if they would like to be on your email or mailing list. This will give them an opportunity to read about new developments in your company and keep your company in their mind.

Statistical Evidence

From a respected source, statistical evidence is a powerful tool. "Nine out of ten dentists agree . . ." is used by a major toothpaste manufacturer. Use statistics backed by an authorized source to prove the effectiveness of your product or service.

The Woman's Advantage

When using visual tools such as business cards, websites and newsletters to promote your product or service, it is worth remembering that female audiences prefer softer colors such as lavender, pink and light blue. Male audiences prefer stronger colors like royal blue, black and forest green.

The female market tends to be attracted to rounded shapes. The male market is generally attracted by sharper edges such as squares or rectangles. Look at products in stores and their packaging. Women's perfumes generally have bottles that are curvy and are either softer colors or dramatic reds and purples.

Products intended for male audiences typically have darker colors in their logos. Male colognes, for example, are not packaged in pastel colors. They are black, brown or navy blue and the bottles are typically square in shape.

If your market includes both genders, you will need to find a balance.

"Trust your hunches. They're usually based
on facts filed away just below the conscious level."
~ Dr. Joyce Brothers

3. Vision

Instruments that provide foresight.

Vision can be achieved by asking well-crafted questions. If a question on your survey encourages buyers to share their innermost feelings, you can be assured that you have made an impact on them.

Vision is effective to help clients in Level 2 Think and Level 3 Plan to move up to the next Level.

Surveys and Scoring

Buyers in Level 2 Think and Level 3 Plan are assessing the pros and cons of their situation. They are picturing themselves doing things differently. Therefore, they may be open to completing a short questionnaire if it will tell them immediately that they should move forward with their problem-solving efforts or stay still. Multiple-choice surveys in magazines are good example.

In-depth Assessments

It is recommended that you always conduct an assessment with your clients to understand their current situation. Use a five minute questionnaire for clients who are in Level 2 Think. Clients who are in Level 3 Plan will be open to a more in-depth set of questions that could take up to 20 minutes to complete.

A short Needs Assessment is a good tool to have on your website. Follow up with a brief telephone conversation to review their responses and provide them with a quick analysis of their current situation with recommendations.

Paid Diagnostics

Some clients in Level 3 Plan are willing to invest their money to thoroughly investigate the perfect solution for their company. Diagnostics should provide Decision Makers with a complete understanding of their situation and your recommended solutions.

Case Studies

Case studies are a detailed illustration of your success with an existing client. They contain four parts: the client's name (the more well-known the better), the situation the client was in, the solution your company provided and the results within a specific period of time.

Product Catalogues

Be aware of how your audience likes to receive information. Is it over the Internet with a user friendly e-commerce store, or is it a four-color printed catalogue hand delivered? Avon and Mary Kay have both – but originally they depended exclusively on their print catalogues.

The Woman's Advantage

Among owners of firms with annual sales of $1 million or more, 58 percent of women say the Internet plays a "moderately or extremely important" role in their growth strategies, while only 35 percent of men say the same. Likewise, 56 percent of the businesses owned by these women have websites that can fulfill transactions online, compared with 38 percent of such enterprises owned by men.[24]

"I think it's always best to be who you are."
~ Halle Berry, actress

4. Emotion

Media that evoke feelings.

Emotion is a powerful method for clients in Level 2 Think. Appeal to the five senses. Advertisers know that photos of human faces yield a higher response rate than pictures of buildings. Colors also influence audiences. Scratch and sniff used in magazines and catalogues is an image evoking invention.

Emotion is an effective Method of Inspiration with clients who are in Level 2 Think and Level 3 Plan.

Video Clips

A video can change someone's mind in an instant. The popularity of YouTube.com demonstrates this. A video does not have to cost a fortune to be effective. Test your video with a small and honest audience first, then post it on the web and invite everyone to see it.

Testimonials

An emotional testimonial will appeal to clients in Level 2 Think and Level 3 Plan. In your promotional material, have a compelling and concise testimonial from a client stating how your services have affected that person's life or business.

Letters of Reference

Clients who are in Level 2 Think or Level 3 Plan are seeking peer credibility. They respond well to letters of reference with emotionally arousing words and statistical evidence. Credibility helps to relieve the sensation of anxiety.

Success Stories

People like to hear true stories that illustrate triumph over adversity. Have success stories on your website and in your marketing material. Include photographs of people who are experiencing the results of your solution.

5. Commitment

Tools that demonstrate a promise to take action.

Clients in Level 3 Plan, Level 4 Do and Level 5 Buy are willing to commit. They are ready to separate themselves from their hard-earned money.

Payment

Buyers in Level 3 Plan do not have allocated funds. They may, however, be willing to invest a percentage of the total investment if it will help them clearly forecast the funds required. Payment for exploratory work, like a test, is a demonstration of commitment.

Pilot or Phase 1

"Pilot" is a term used quite often in business. We suggest you use the term "Phase 1" instead, as pilot can imply that the project may or may not "fly."

Phase 1 is perfect for clients who are willing to invest a percentage of the purchase price to see you in action. When they can see the benefits they will usually continue with Phase 2.

Provision of Action Plan or Business Plan

Ask to see a copy of your client's action plan or business plan. Providing you with this information can be a good indication of trust and partnership. If your client doesn't have a business plan, you can offer to help develop one for a fee.

Meeting with All Decision Makers

A demonstration of commitment is a meeting with *all* the Decision Makers that you have identified on your Interaction Scorecard. Its purpose could be to conduct an in-depth assessment or participate in your proposal presentation. Either way, the objective is to discuss the recommended solutions and come to an agreement on how to move forward.

Non-Disclosure Agreement (NDA)

A client may ask you to sign a NDA. This helps to protect their corporate secrets. You may be invited to sign a mutual NDA that would protect both you and your client.

Don't hesitate to have your legal counsel review it before you sign. In fact, it's better if you and your legal counsel develop your own NDA and have the client sign it.

Contractual Agreement

Unless you have a very complicated offering try to keep your contractual agreement down to one page. Put all the terms and conditions for the successful delivery of your solution in your proposal. The details of the agreement should refer back to the details in the proposal.

> *Hint:*   *Have legal representation review any document that you are asked to sign. Signing the contractual agreement is a form of commitment. Make sure you get the money at the same time. In most countries, contracts are binding only if money is exchanged.*

Invoices

Always present an invoice that clearly states your company's full legal name, your mailing address, your telephone number and your website address. Every piece of paper from your company is an opportunity to advertise. Also include on your invoice your tax numbers, your payment terms and a "thank you for doing business with us."

Credit Cards

Make is easier for your clients to commit by accepting established credit cards for payment. Your banker can help set this up for you. Yes, there is a small fee but it is worth it since the money is deposited directly into your bank account.

6. Replacement

Substitution for past or present behaviour.

Clients in Level 4 Do may not know what the new solution will look like. Clients in Level 5 Buy need to experience customer satisfaction before they can be relieved of their buyer's remorse. Clients who continue to use your solution will successfully rise up to Level 6 Believe.

Guarantees

Assure your clients that they are making the right decision. Buyer's remorse can set in as early as Level 4 Do, especially before they are about to sign the contract. A "100% Satisfaction Guarantee" may relieve some of the pressure.

Free Delivery

You can encourage clients to buy more quickly when you offer free delivery for the first order. Then share your policy for subsequent deliveries.

Buy More, Then Get a Discount

Lack of perceived value, not price, is usually the issue when your clients have not yet committed. Provide discounts only when your client is willing to give something back. For instance, consider offering volume discounts. Costco built an empire on this concept. You could take it a step further and offer a "preferred client" price list.

Demonstrations

Provide a demonstration of how your product works. The goal is to encourage your clients to try your products so that they will replace what they are currently using. For example, having a client test drive a car can inspire a person to purchase it.

Standing Orders

Long-term clients appreciate it when you anticipate their needs. Standing orders are items that can be shipped out to your clients on a pre-set delivery schedule. This is a terrific way to ensure cash flow for your company.

Samples

Giving your clients a sample of your product is a great way to introduce a new product. Procter & Gamble still mails little packets of Tide to neighborhoods with household incomes that are higher than average, because it is one of the more expensive laundry soaps on the market.

"I am extraordinarily patient,
provided I get my own way in the end."
~ Margaret Thatcher, Prime Minister
United Kingdom, 1979-1990

7. Environment

Change in physical surroundings.

Environment is an effective inspiration Method for Decision Makers in Level 4 Do to move to Level 5 Buy. It also helps clients in Level 5 Buy become raving fans.

Leisure Activities

For years, golf has been used to conduct business. For those of you who don't golf, there are alternatives such as sailing, skiing, tennis, or any leisure activity that you and your clients enjoy. This time and close proximity will help to build a more personal relationship with them.

Site Visits

Take Decision Makers to the site of one of your clients in Level 6 Believe and show them how your product or service is being used. Have your clients provide testimonials and statistics proving how your solution increased productivity, reduced costs and increased profits. Other benefits may include improved staff morale and decreased staff absenteeism.

Hint: *Take a potential client for a site visit after you've conducted an in-depth Needs Assessment or a paid diagnostic to ensure that the site visit is relevant to them.*

Lunch

Arrange a lunch after the site visit to assess the client's Level of Interest. Come prepared with your proposal, the contractual agreement and the invoice, just in case the client responds positively and is prepared to sign the deal.

Office Visits

Whether you are visiting your client's office or your client is visiting you, consider sitting around a coffee table or a small boardroom table. Sitting behind a desk implies a higher status.

8. Reward

Acknowledgment for positive behaviour.

Success will increase when you reward people for positive behavior. It will also encourage the repetition of that behavior. Clients in Level 4 Do, Level 5 Buy and Level 6 Believe respond well to Reward.

Small Gifts

The value of a gift for a client in Level 4 Do should be modest. If a gift is offered too early or if it is too big, it can be construed as a bribe or an obligation to do business. Some companies have clearly written policies regarding the acceptance of gifts. These policies may state that gifts cannot be received by employees, or that there is a maximum value that cannot be exceeded. Depending on the company's policy, give gifts as a reward for positive behavior.

Hint: *It is important to know the culturally acceptable behavior surrounding gift-giving for each country, industry or company that you are dealing with when considering suitable Rewards.*

Exceed Expectations

Exceeding your client's expectations, just slightly, will help to retain a client without cutting into your profit margin. For example, if it is convenient for the client, deliver just slightly before the deadlines you set.

Time

Give your clients the gift of time by setting up meetings for an hour but get your business done within 45 minutes. There's no sweeter sound to a Decision Makers' ears than, "There are 15 minutes to spare, is there anything else we need to discuss?" Ask for the order, set up the next appointment, say your good-byes and get out of their way.

Gift Certificates

Since women are the major purchasers of household items it is estimated that women use gift certificates more than men. Ensure that your clients want the rewards you offer. Consider factors such as their interests, age, marital status and whether or not they have children. Treat your clients as individuals and reward them as such.

Membership

Consider what kinds of benefits you could offer buyers for becoming a member of an elite club with your company. Benefits of membership could include discounts on future purchases, exclusive products and services or guest invitations to special events. Can you partner with other companies to offer more significant rewards that will benefit your clients? Rewards could include discounts on car rentals, hotel accommodations or office supplies.

"Nothing will work unless you do."
~ Dr. Maya Angelo, author

9. Help

Instruments that provide assistance.

Clients in Level 4 Do are ready to buy. Make it easy for them. For instance, clients should be able to contact you during business hours. Depending on your industry, you may need an after-hours emergency contact number. If buyers have difficulty contacting you, they may contact your competition instead.

Use the following tools to inspire clients in Level 4 Do to commit and clients who are in Levels 5 Buy and Level 6 Believe, to stay.

Technical Sales Support

In some organizations, the salesperson may not have the technical expertise to answer more specific questions about the solution they represent. In-house technical experts can help facilitate the sales process by offering expert advice.

Online Support

Some challenges can be resolved online. IBM and Hewlett-Packard pioneered the offering of online help supported by on-demand telephone support.

Toll-Free Help Line

Enable your clients to call long distance for free by setting up a toll-free number. It costs a lot less than you think. Connect the number to a help desk or have it forwarded to your cell phone. Either way, they won't hesitate to dial.

Training

More and more solutions require training for clients to experience the full benefit of products and services. Ensure your clients are scheduled for training at a time that suits their schedule. Consider on-site or off-site training, whichever is most convenient for them. Leave them with easy to understand reference manuals or instructions on-line.

Service Contracts

Ensure your clients are clear about how they will be taken care of after they have purchased from you. Sears has built a separate business by providing service on the appliances they sell. Consider offering your clients added-value service contracts that they can pay extra for.

The Woman's Advantage

Women tend to thrive in supportive, caring relationships and sometimes create semi-personal business relationships, unlike men who tend to have more casual, less personal business relationships. Provide the level of assistance that is expected by your clients and ensure you get paid for it.[25]

"There's an assumption that 'negotiation' means 'battle,'
or that it's got to be 'intense' or 'tense.' I always like to use humour. There's
something funny about everything.
At the most tense moments, I like to bring everyone back
and let their humanness catch up."
~ Jeanne Coughlin, The Rise of Women Entrepreneurs

The Application of The Nine Methods

Not all clients come into our lives at Level 1 Exist. They could be in Level 2 Think, Level 3 Plan, or Level 4 Do. They come to us in different Levels of Interest. When we are engaged with them, they can move up and down the Levels, right before our eyes.

To quickly determine your client's Level of Interest use the Four Keys in the Interaction Scorecard and your customized Interaction Questionnaire. Then use the Methods of Inspiration that best relate to their particular Level of Interest.

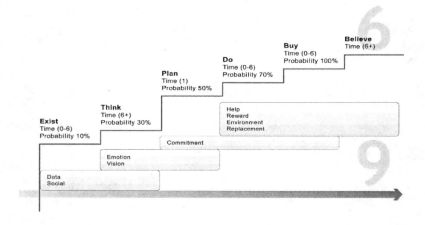

Clients in Level 1 Exist respond best to Social and Data Methods of Inspiration. Clients in Level 2 Think are positively affected by Social, Data, Vision and Emotion. Clients in Level 3 Plan respond best to Vision, Emotion and Commitment. Clients in Level 4 Do take action when Commitment, Replacement, Environment, Reward and Help are presented to them.

A powerful Method of Inspiration used at the wrong Level of Interest can de-motivate a client. This can waste both your and their valuable time and resources.

To inspire future clients to become buyers create a personalized menu of tools translated from each of The Nine Methods of Inspiration.

"All change is not growth,
as all movement is not forward."
~ Ellen Glasgow, American novelist

Level 1 Exist

Social and Data Methods of Inspiration will inspire a client in
Level 1 Exist to Level 2 Think.

 www.SellingforWomen.com

Method	Level 1 Exist
Social **Legislative or cultural laws that affect behavior.**	Legislative Laws Industry Standards Third Party Test Results Goods Sold at Cost Referrals
Data **Information that increases awareness.**	Advertising Brochures Mailing Lists Statistical Evidence

Remember to consider gender differences when personalizing
your Data tools. For products aimed at women, use the word
"reliability" and cite sizes and colors. For products aimed at men,
use words such as "power," "torque," and "speed."

For services aimed at women, cite references and use words such
as "flexibility," "customizable," and "reputation." For services
aimed at men, state dates, statistics and prices.

Level 2 Think

To inspire a client in Level 2 Think to move up to Level 3 Plan, use tools translated from Social, Data, Vision and Emotion Methods of Inspiration.

   www.SellingforWomen.com

Method	Level 2 Think
Social Legislative or cultural laws that affect behavior.	Legislative Laws Industry Standards Test Results Goods Sold at Cost Referrals
Data Information that increases awareness.	Advertising Brochures Mailing Lists Statistical Evidence
Vision Instruments that provide foresight.	Surveys with Scores In-depth Assessments Paid Diagnostics Case Studies Product Catalogues
Emotion Media that evoke feelings.	Video Clips Testimonials Letters of Reference Success Stories

Level 3 Plan

Use Vision, Emotion and Commitment, in this order, with buyers who are in Level 3 Plan.

  www.SellingforWomen.com

Method	Level 3 Plan
Vision Instruments that provide foresight.	Surveys with Scores In-depth Assessments Paid Diagnostics Case Studies Product Catalogues
Emotion Media that evoke feelings.	Video Clips Testimonials Letters of Reference Success Stories
Commitment Tools that demonstrate a promise to take action.	Deposit Phase 1 Action Plan Meeting with Decision Makers Non-Disclosure Agreement Proposal Contract Invoice

Level 4 Do

Your client is only one stage away from Level 5 Buy! Luckily, you have the most Methods available than any other in the buying process. Use Commitment, Replacement, Environment, Reward and Help in this order.

 www.SellingforWomen.com

Method	Level 4 Do
Commitment Tools that demonstrate a promise to take action.	Deposit Meeting with Decision Makers Proposal Contract Invoice
Replacement Substitution for past or present behavior.	Guarantee Free Delivery Warranty Volume Discount Demonstration Standing Order Sample
Environment Change in physical surroundings.	Leisure Activity Site Visit Office Visit Lunch

www.SellingforWomen.com

Method	Level 4 Do
Reward **Acknowledgment for positive behavior.**	Small Gift Exceed Expectations Time Membership
Help **Instruments that provide assistance.**	Technical Sales Support Online Support Toll-Free Help Line Training

Heads up!   *If you have a client that you have assessed at Level 4 Do and you have not yet conducted a Needs Assessment, then do so. Then reward them for completing this fundamental task with an in-depth analysis, a proposal for resolution and the bill.*

Level 5 Buy

In Level 5 Buy, you have access to the same five Methods of Inspiration as you did for clients who are in Level 4 Do. At every Level different challenges and concerns come up. This is the reason for having specific tools for each Level of Interest. The more tools you have available, the quicker you can resolve your client's issues.

 www.SellingforWomen.com

Method	Level 5 Buy
Commitment	100% Paid In Full
Replacement Substitution for past or present behavior.	Warranty Free Delivery Standing Order
Environment Change in physical surroundings.	Leisure Activity Site Visit Office Visit Lunch
Reward Acknowledgment for positive behavior.	Small Gift Exceed Expectations Time Membership
Help Instruments that provide assistance.	Technical Sales Support Online Support Toll-Free Help Line Training

Level 6 Believe

Clients are advocates when they continually purchase from you, rave about your solutions to others and provide you with referrals. They no longer require tools derived from Commitment. However, they require Replacement, Environment, Reward and Help to maintain this Level of Interest.

   www.SellingforWomen.com

Method	Level 6 Believe
Replacement Substitution for past or present behavior.	Guarantee Free Delivery Warranty Standing Order
Environment Change in physical surroundings.	Leisure Activity Site Visit Office Visit Dinner
Reward Acknowledgment for positive behavior.	Client Appreciation Events Exceed Expectations Time Free Membership Special Customer Pricing
Help Instruments that provide assistance.	Free Online Support Toll-Free Help Line Training Referrals to Grow Their Business

The Woman's Advantage

Author and psychologist Carl Rogers said, "People perceive things differently due to differences in cultural and ethnic background, personal experiences, personality styles, gender differences, attitudes and beliefs. This diversity may impact our ability to communicate with each other."

A deeper awareness of how women and men communicate differently from one another will prevent you from losing sales and alienating clients due to gender differences.

Research indicates that women and men are socialized differently and consequently, have different styles of speaking. Deborah Tannen calls the differences "rapport talk" versus "report talk."[26] Women tend to use "rapport talk" to establish intimacy and connection while men tend to use "report talk" to convey information and self-importance. In a sales or a client service environment, these differences impact the way messages are sent and received, often causing communication breakdown, misunderstanding and major frustration. The gender differences can also create inconsistent communication with potential clients.

Research is confirming that women's and men's brains are somewhat different. Certain areas in a woman's brain contain more nerve cells and can transfer information quickly back and forth from the left to the right side of her brain. This is why women can be both logical and emotional at the same time. Men tend to be either one or the other.[27]

Although none of these findings shows superiority, they illustrate that women and men are made differently, with different needs and different ideas. Generally, women bond and communicate well in one-to-one conversations and in groups.

Women tend to interact face-to-face, such as when sitting in a living room or having an office discussion. Men bond best with friends or their children while engaging in an activity instead of speaking face-to-face.

The following table lists some of the stereotypical and potentially controversial perspectives about communication differences between women and men.

Women	Men
Conversation is an interaction	Conversation is an exchange of information
Friendship is common secrets	Friendship is teamwork
A good communicator stares wide-eyed, listens actively, says "really?" and forgets about her surroundings	A good communicator is someone who can listen to you and give valuable advice when asked for
Listening to a man's monologue is tedious, but useful	Listening to a woman's monologue means being subservient to her

These traits are commonly believed to be true for all women and all men.

During the 2008 American Democratic race between Hillary Clinton and Barack Obama, rumors were that many Americans in office, both Republican and Democrats, would prefer to see Obama get the Democratic seat rather than Clinton because they did not want to have to report to a woman. That would mean having to listen to a woman's monologue, meaning they were "beneath" her. Yes, this prejudice still exists, but just seeing

Hillary Clinton get to the level she rose to, was inspiring for all women.

"Looking at female [political] candidates today,
other women are the hardest on them,
especially older women who were brought up in a different culture."
~ Eleanor Clift,
American political commentator/writer

An awareness of nonverbal communication is integral in sales, all the way from conducting your Level of Interest assessment to negotiating a win-win solution. Clients often say more with body language, such as personal space required, gestures and eye contact, than with actual words. An obvious example is someone saying "yes" verbally while turning their face left and right, indicating "no."

What's interesting is that men will provide different "signals" than women. A research study conducted at Valdosta State University[28] determined gender differences in several areas of nonverbal communication. Specifically, the areas of eye contact, gestures, smiles, personal space, touch and interpretation of non-verbal cues were examined.

Which gender established more eye contact? It was concluded that North American women engage in more eye contact during conversations than men. Women, more often in a subordinate role, make more eye contact than a person in a dominant position. In addition, the study found that women are more comfortable giving eye contact than are men. This should be a factor to consider before you get discouraged or frustrated if a man is not able to look you in the eye often or for long. This behavior does not necessarily mean that the sales call did not go well.

Which gender used more gestures? The stereotype believed by both women and men was that women use more gestures than men. However, the opinions of experts were mixed. Some scientists felt that women used fewer gestures than men. They also stated that women use fewer gestures when they are with other women, but more gestures when they are with men. It was felt that the difference was in the types of gestures used rather than in the frequency of use.

Which gender smiled more often? Not only did women smile more than men, but they were also more attracted to others who smiled. Almost everyone surveyed said they would automatically return a smile if someone smiled at them first. Since women tend to smile more, the sales interaction can feel less formal. Since men tend to smile less, the sales interaction can seem more formal, until you smile and influence them to smile.

Which gender required more personal space? Fifty-six percent of the female respondents felt they require more personal space than a male. However, all the experts agreed that males use more personal space than females.

Which gender touched more in business? For years women did not shake other women's hands and men did not shake women's hands. Women merely nodded and smiled to acknowledge one another and they are comfortable in personal relationships where hugging is accepted.

Women don't shake hands with their mother or their friends. Men shake hands with their father, friends and business associates. In the Western hemisphere today, shaking hands is a common act, regardless of gender.

Which gender was able to interpret nonverbal cues better? Experts agreed that females are better interpreters of nonverbal cues. Scientists described women as being more sensitive communicators and more astute to nonverbal cues. They concluded that women more actively communicate the importance of relationships by using a number of verbal and nonverbal channels.

Be secure in the knowledge that women are natural born sales professionals.

Lisa's Story

Lisa obtained her real estate license when she realized that her love of architecture and interior design could be combined with sales. She had a successful practice, but things changed when she married and had her first child. Now she had something else that demanded her limited time, of which she was more than happy to give, but not at the expense of her income.

She realized quickly that things had to get a lot more streamlined, both at home and at work, if she was to continue her comfortable lifestyle and ensure her family's happiness, so she decided to apply:

The Three Steps to
LifestyleSelling

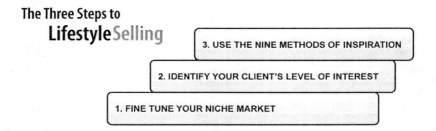

3. USE THE NINE METHODS OF INSPIRATION

2. IDENTIFY YOUR CLIENT'S LEVEL OF INTEREST

1. FINE TUNE YOUR NICHE MARKET

The first thing she did was conduct a market analysis of her current clients. She learned that they were all referrals, some single, sixty-eight percent were married, between the ages of twenty-eight and forty-five and earned above average incomes.

She also discovered that forty-two percent of her clients lived within ten miles of each other. This was her Niche Market.

She then conducted a survey and found out that her clients had many challenges. She realized that she needed to position herself as a specialist to address these challenges.

She was now ready to actively seek out clients that fit her Niche Market profile. Instead of relying on word-of-mouth alone, she started to advertise weekly in the local newspapers that catered to her ideal clients. These ads included her best photograph.

When she discovered that a growing number of her clients were buying second and third properties for rental income purposes, she began to advertise and conduct rental property seminars. Her website was revamped to show a more personal touch, instead of being associated with a huge company where "any agent might do."

She made sure that the same photograph that was used in her newspaper ads was posted on the home page of her website. After sixteen weeks, people that she met for the first time would smile and say, "I know you. You look familiar." She marketed her *"How-to buy, make money and profit from rental property"* seminars through Facebook.com and Linkedin.com.

Lisa published a separate homepage on Facebook.com to show the more personal side of her wonderful life. She invested in Salesforce.com, the web-based customer relationship management software to keep track of all her existing and future clients. She tracked her marketing campaigns through Salesforce.com and measured the return on her advertising investment.

She printed smart and attractive brochures and business cards to leave with clients and other realtors. She offered an electronic newsletter to her existing and near-buying clients filled with tips and tricks to successful homeownership and rentals. She hired an assistant part time to send out little holiday cards to her clients handwritten with a heartfelt note. She built a marketing machine to ensure that she would be remembered and enable her to find high quality future clients.

Bonnie and Paul met Lisa at a networking event hosted by the business club they all belong to. They were getting married in a year and they decided to buy a home together. Bonnie remembered seeing Lisa's advertisements for her monthly seminars in the local community newspaper. They hit it off right away. Bonnie and Paul gushed as they told Lisa why they intended to buy a house before they were married, one that they could call "their own."

Lisa explained how important it was for her to completely understand what they were looking for, before she recommended any properties, as she did not wish to waste any of their valuable time. Bonnie and Paul agreed. They exchanged business cards and agreed to review their "dream home requirements."

Using her customized Interaction Questionnaire, Lisa was able to privately complete an Interaction Scorecard. She uncovered that there were other people involved in the purchase. Bonnie's mother would be contributing to the down-payment and Paul's best friend was a city planner who had his fingers on the pulse of the municipal changes.

Lisa also discovered during the forty-five minute analysis that their ideal home had to have a garden, three bedrooms and two baths.

They wanted to live within 20 minutes from Paul's place of work. With the help of Bonnie's mother they had enough down-payment and pre-authorized mortgage money to buy the house of their dreams in the neighborhood that they desired.

As for timing, if they didn't find the perfect house before the wedding, Bonnie said it would break her heart. Paul said it didn't matter to him and that they would just keep looking.

Bonnie was the most keen to make a decision. As far as she was concerned, they were buying a house. Paul, on the other hand, didn't think that the world would come to an end if they didn't find a house before they became husband and wife. Bonnie's mother had her hands on the purse strings. Without her down payment, they could not afford to live in their preferred neighborhood. Because Bonnie's mother was not involved in the conversation with Lisa, Lisa knew that she was going to have to rate this Opportunity as a Level 1 with a 10 percent chance to close.

Lisa asked Bonnie and Paul if they would be available to look at properties during the week. Thinking about their heavy schedules, they said that after work would prove to be impossible. Lisa suggested that they meet again next Saturday and that she would have some properties for them to view. They agreed. Then she said to Bonnie, "Why don't you bring your mother along?" Without looking at her fiancé, Bonnie squealed, "What a great idea. I'll call her right now." Eager to please, Paul agreed.

Over three weekends they viewed twenty-two properties. Gently and methodically, Lisa took them through the buying process. First she established credibility with Bonnie's mother, pointing out that her family belonged to the same club. They talked of her fourteen years in real estate and she listened while Bonnie's mother regaled her in tales of owning her own business for thirty years.

She helped the couple to envision the life they could have in the various homes that they visited and silently watched as Bonnie's mother fantasized about cooking for her daughter while baby-to-be slept in the nursery upstairs.

Lisa encouraged them to commit by asking her mother point-blank, "When these two find the home of their dreams, is there anything that could stop them?" There were no real issues. Lisa did all she could to simplify the buying process.

Whenever needed, she provided them with a tape measure so they could determine if their existing furniture would fit. She listened while they spoke about how their current place was "too small" and she supported them when they put their first offer on a home.

She held Bonnie's hand when the deal fell through and continued to show them more homes. She sent them emails of listings, presented comparable homes and informed them of city ordinances.

Before the wedding, the critical deadline in Bonnie's mind, Lisa was successful in helping the couple find their dream home.

Bonnie and Paul have since referred Lisa to their friends and have stated that they will definitely have Lisa assist them should they choose to relocate.

All in all, a happy ending.

Get Involved

We bring professional women together to provide each other continued support and positive outcomes.

It is an effective way to meet new contacts and share your vision.

We invite you to join the *Selling for Women* Network.

By getting involved, you will expand your network, interact with women in business and create new opportunities.

www.SellingforWomen.com/Network

Call us Toll FREE at 1-800-681-7808

"Too much of a good thing is wonderful."
~ Mae West, actress

Ongoing Learning

Because your success is our success we make it easy for you to get the support you need to overcome specific challenges.

Our solutions include:

- One-on-One Personal Coaching
- Customized Workshops and Seminars
- Webinars
- Retreats
- Corporate Consulting

Our solutions provide the path for increased revenues and ensure the future value of your business.

www.SellingforWomen.com/Solutions

Call us Toll FREE at **1-800-681-7808**

About the Authors

Pauline O'Malley

Pauline's passion is sales. As an entrepreneur and as a top producer, Pauline's career spans the retail, education, insurance and technology sectors. Foreseeing a more holistic approach to selling, Pauline embarked upon the development of a system that would integrate marketing, sales and customer service. In 2002, after three and a half years of testing with 260 companies and individuals, she and her company published *TheRevenueBuilder®* – *Making Customer Relationship Management Work!*

In 2004, Pauline co-authored *Win Without Pitching* with Blair Enns for the communications and advertising sector. In 2006, Pauline, Blair Enns and Cal Harrison co-produced *Beyond Referrals* for management consultants and professional services firms. Today, she and her team of strategists travel throughout North America, Europe, China and India assisting clients with the 9th edition of *TheRevenueBuilder®* – *The Elements.*

Pauline is a sought after keynote speaker. Her unabashed honesty, quick sense of humor and practical advice generates action that results in increased revenues.

Pauline is also a tireless volunteer, currently involved in the support of political candidates. She is the Founding Chair of the nationally acclaimed Leaders of Tomorrow Mentorship Program with the Vancouver Board of Trade and received the Chairman's award for excellence in leadership.

Born in the United States, Pauline lives in Canada with homes on the beach in Toronto, Vancouver and Pender Island.

Brenda Page, CPC

Since the age of eleven, when she was presented with the news that she might not survive open-heart surgery, Brenda Page has dedicated her life to contributing to others. Her mission is to awaken, enlighten and inspire individuals to live every moment 'on purpose' and 'not by accident'. Brenda is also the founder of Crystal Clear Concepts established in 1992. Her moving philosophies have been published in *Women Who Speak, Speak Out* and O, The Oprah Magazine.

As an Internationally Certified Life and Business Coach (CPC), Brenda helps individuals and teams break through barriers that impede personal and professional growth. Whatever her client's challenge; dealing with transition in their personal life, career changes, leadership challenges or business issues, Brenda's coaching assists them to fulfill their goals.

Brenda is also a Certified Train the Trainer and a powerful keynote speaker. By applying her extensive human resources background, Brenda custom designs workshops and training programs for corporations, private business, associations and government on a wide variety of topics. Her solutions blend practical advice with tools that can be implemented immediately, creating absolutely impressive results.

Brenda was born in Connecticut, U.S.A. and spent most of her schooling years in New Brunswick, Canada. She has recently returned to New Brunswick after living for twenty years in Vancouver, British Columbia. She volunteers with numerous organizations such as Unicef, The David Foster Foundation and Abused Women's Groups.

References

1. *The Power of the Purse,* Fara Warner, ISBN 0131855190

2. *Selling Power Magazine,* 2008

3. *NonPareil Inc,* 2008

4. *Center for Women's Business Research,* 2006

5. *Real Business Magazine,* 2008

6. *The Center for Women's Business Research,* 2006

7. *Inc.com,* 2007

8. *Key Facts About Women-Owned Businesses,* 2008

9. *Center for Women's Business Research,* 2006

10. *Center for Women's Business Research,* 2007

11. *Key Facts About Women-Owned Businesses,* 2008

12. *Center for Women's Business Research,* 2007

13. *Center for Women's Business Research,* 2007

14. *CIBC Report on Women-Owned Business in Canada,* 2004

15. *National Foundation for Women Business Owners,* 2006

16. *Key Facts About Women-Owned Businesses,* 2008

17. *CIBC Report on Women-Owned Business in Canada,* 2004

18. *CIBC Report on Women-Owned Business in Canada*, 2004

19. *Center for Women's Business Research*, November 2006

20. *Changing for Good*, Prochaska, James O., Norcross, John C. & DiClemente, Carlo C., ISBN: 0688112633

21. *America's Competitive Secret: Women Managers*, Judy Rosener, ISBN 0195119142

22. *The Dealix Dealer Newsletter*, March 2006

23. *CNW Marketing Research*, 2006

24. *Center for Women's Business Research*, 2007

25. *National Foundation for Women Business Owners*, 2006

26. *You Just Don't Understand: Women and Men in Conversation*, Deborah Tannen, ISBN 0060959622

27. *86th Scientific Assembly and Annual Meeting of the Radiological Society of North America*, November 2002

28. *Valdosta State University in Valdosta, Georgia research study in 1998 reviewed previous studies conducted by* Burgoon, Buller and Woodall (1996), Ivy and Backlund (1994), Hanna and Wilson (1994/1996)